To the women of Rosie's Place
CM

To all those who dedicate their lives to helping others
VT-K

Text copyright © 2022 by Christine McDonnell
Illustrations copyright © 2022 by Victoria Tentler-Krylov

First edition 2022

Library of Congress Catalog Card Number pending
ISBN 978-1-5362-1129-0

21 22 23 24 25 26 APS 10 9 8 7 6 5 4 3 2 1

Printed in Humen, Dongguan, China

This book was typeset in ITC Veljovic.
The illustrations were created with watercolor and digital media.

Candlewick Press
99 Dover Street
Somerville, Massachusetts 02144

www.candlewick.com

Sanctuary

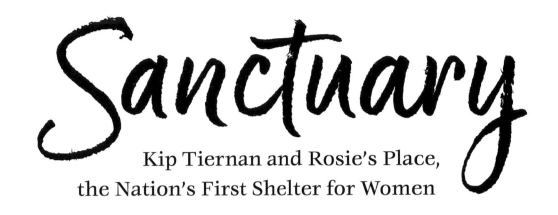

Kip Tiernan and Rosie's Place,
the Nation's First Shelter for Women

Christine McDonnell

illustrated by Victoria Tentler-Krylov

CANDLEWICK PRESS

KIP stood on tiptoe to stir the big pot of soup on Granny's stove. Already men were lining up by the back door, collars turned up and shoulders hunched against the cold. Some blew on their hands to keep them warm. Granny ladled the soup, and Kip carried the steaming bowls outside.

It was during the Great Depression of the 1930s, when many people lost their savings, jobs, and even their homes. Men, women, and children begged on street corners for money or food. Some left chalk marks on the sidewalk as guides for other needy people. The mark outside Granny's house signaled that it was a good, safe place to be fed.

After Kip's father died when she was an infant, Kip was raised in Granny's house. She was named Mary Jane after both grandmothers, but everyone called her Kippie.

With many of her ten children living at home, Kip's grandmother already had plenty of people to feed. But she always gave food to those who knocked on her kitchen door. She gave whatever she could. When a man needed shoes, she gave away a pair belonging to her son. She even gave away a shaving kit. In her grandmother's kitchen, Kip learned to be generous and to care about others.

"Why are we feeding those men, Granny?" Kip asked. "We don't even know them."

"I don't have to know them to know that they're hungry, that they're good men who have come upon hard times," her grandmother said. "We're a lot better off than the people who come to our door."

WHEN she became an adult, Kip practiced the lessons she learned in her grandmother's kitchen. In 1968 she heard speakers call for change in America, urging people to help bring an end to poverty and war. Listening, Kip said she "passed through a door and there is no turning back." She sold her advertising business and joined the staff at Warwick House, in a poor neighborhood of Boston.

At Warwick House, if you were hungry, you could get a meal. You could find someone to listen. You could come there to pray. The workers at Warwick House visited jails and prisons. They helped kids in trouble. They gave out food and even money for rent. The door at 1 Warwick Street was always open.

One night Kip was serving food to a line of hungry people. As she dished stew onto plates, she saw that the last person in line was a slim figure with small hands—a woman dressed in men's clothes. After this, Kip noticed other women dressed as men, always at the back of the line. At that time, shelters were only for men. Women had to disguise themselves to get a meal and a bed.

As she walked through the city, Kip noticed more homeless women: women on park benches, wearing layers of clothes; women searching for food in trash cans; women sleeping in doorways and bus stations; women with shopping baskets filled with all their belongings.

Just as her grandmother had helped people during the Depression, Kip was determined to help these homeless women. She asked city officials and the people in charge of shelters why there was no help for these women. Again and again, she heard this answer: homelessness isn't a women's problem.

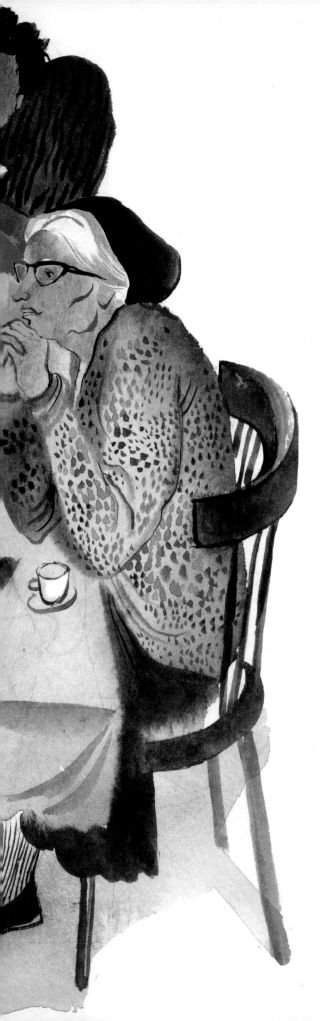

Kip visited other cities and found few places where women could go for help. But at Saint Joseph's House of Hospitality, in New York City, Dorothy Day opened the door to anyone in need. Kip spent three weeks there.

At Saint Joseph's House, everyone ate together. Kip looked down the row of people seated at the long table. Individuals struggling with addiction or living with mental illness were among the guests. Sometimes, at dinner, the only sentence she understood was "Pass the bread, please." Toward the end of her stay, she decided to turn and touch people's arms, to look into their eyes, to listen to them. She did this for the next three days.

On the fourth day, when she came down to breakfast, guests from dinner had gathered at the foot of the stairs.

"They're waiting for you," a worker told her.

"Why?" Kip asked, worried that she had done something wrong.

"Because you listened to them," Dorothy Day said.

Kip hoped to open a women's shelter different from the dreary ones she had seen, where men slept with their shoes under their pillows to keep them from being stolen.

She wanted to open a sanctuary with flowers and music where women wouldn't be reminded they were poor, a shelter with no chores, no questions asked, just good meals and warm beds. She hoped the volunteers at her shelter would listen to the guests. When you listen to others, you show respect; you learn who they are and what they need.

For Kip's dream to come true, she needed a building. She visited Boston city officials and urged them to help. They only had to look around to see homeless women in the parks, stations, and libraries— women with nowhere to go. Kip begged; she nagged; she would not give up. Later she said, "Sometimes all you need is just plain stubborn hope."

Finally the city agreed to rent her an empty supermarket in a poor part of town. The price? One dollar a year. Probably they gave her the building to end her pestering. The place had already been empty for a year, and no one was using it. It had been Rosen's Market. Kip wanted a warm, welcoming name that would signal it as a place for women. She called the shelter Rosie's Place.

Rosie's Place opened on Easter Sunday, 1974, with sandwiches and coffee available. Kip and the volunteers distributed leaflets throughout the area inviting women to come. Soon hot meals were served and beds were available.

In a fundraising letter, Kip wrote, "Women can come in here for free meals, free clothes, and can talk, or watch television or play cards, but mostly it's a place they can come to where no one will criticize them for being poor, or dirty, or sick or alone or lonely." It was the first shelter in the country just for women.

Kip was always thinking about the needs of poor and homeless women. In her speeches and her writing, she questioned the way things were: "Who decides who gets the condo and who gets the cardboard box?" She reminded people that "the face of homeless women is our face. She is our mother, our sister, our daughter and she deserves more than three hots and a cot."

She helped to start Boston Health Care for the Homeless to bring doctors to people on the streets and in shelters. She began the Greater Boston Food Bank to distribute food to the poor. She cofounded the Poor People's United Fund to finance programs helping the poor. She fought for permanent housing for the poor and homeless.

One day, years later, she boarded a crowded bus
with a friend. They found seats in the back. The bus
began to move out into traffic but then pulled to the
curb. The driver made his way down the aisle.
He held out his hand to Kip.

"Thank you," he said. "It's because of you that I
ate when I was a child."

MORE ABOUT KIP TIERNAN

A Rebel and an Outsider

As a young rebel who learned to fly and who loved jazz piano, Kip Tiernan (1926–2011) understood what it felt like to be an outsider, and this understanding contributed to her compassion for those experiencing poverty and homelessness. She overcame alcohol addiction in her twenties and was supportive of those who struggled with drug and alcohol addictions.

Kip valued the humanity of the women who came to Rosie's Place and insisted that they be treated with dignity. She refused to accept city, state, or federal funds because she would not keep records of guests, believing that it was disrespectful of their privacy.

The Great Depression

On October 29, 1929, a day known as Black Tuesday, the stock market crashed as stock prices collapsed. The value of investments disappeared in a single day. Banks closed and people lost their savings. Businesses failed, too, causing people to lose their jobs. One in four American workers, more than twelve million, were unemployed and unable to pay their bills or mortgages. In every city, people lined up at soup kitchens for food.

Hoping to find work, men traveled from town to town, city to city, hitchhiking and catching rides on freight trains while dodging the bulls, the guards hired by the railroads. They had to keep moving to avoid the police. Some people went knocking door to door, begging. Flocks of people, mostly men, but women as well, and even children, begged on street corners. They needed a handout of money or food. They needed a meal and a place to sleep. People called them hoboes or tramps.

Hobo Symbols

As hoboes wandered through towns and cities, they left symbols chalked on sidewalks, posts, or doors to guide other wanderers:

> An X meant that a home was a good, safe place for a handout.
> A cat meant "A kind woman lives here."
> Crossed lines below a face meant "There's a doctor here."
> A triangle and a top hat meant that the homeowners were wealthy.
> A pair of shovels meant that the family would provide food in exchange for work.

Causes of Homelessness

Kip Tiernan pushed for solutions to homelessness, insisting on the humanity and dignity of the poor. She understood homelessness to be a result of many factors:

Urban renewal: In the 1960s, cities razed poor neighborhoods to make way for new buildings. When older buildings were destroyed, many people lost their homes. The higher rents in the new buildings forced people from their neighborhoods. Many became homeless.

Gentrification: Wanting to live in the city, people bought buildings in affordable, rundown urban neighborhoods. They renovated homes and improved the areas, making the houses more valuable and the neighborhoods more expensive to live in. Poor people could not afford to stay and were forced out.

Deinstitutionalization: Large institutions for the mentally ill were closed in a reform movement meant to improve the treatment of people with mental illness. These were to be replaced by small group homes, but only a few existed and those that opened could house only a fraction of those in need. Many people with mental illness had nowhere to go and became homeless.

Veterans' trauma: Many soldiers who served in the Vietnam War returned home with problems such as drug addiction and post-traumatic stress disorder (PTSD). They were unable to work and joined the homeless population.

Drug and alcohol addiction: Alcohol addiction led to poverty and homelessness for many decades. Drug addiction increased the ranks of the homeless in the second half of the twentieth century.

Kip Tiernan Memorial

A memorial to Kip Tiernan was unveiled in October 2018, near Copley Square, in Boston. Tall arches inscribed with quotations from Kip Tiernan's speeches and writing line the sidewalk. The arches represent doorways, an image that Kip Tiernan frequently used to explain her decision to join the urban ministry at Warwick House: "I have passed through a door and there is no turning back."

The quotations on the memorial include the following:

"Cui Bono? Who sets the terms of the debate around poverty and homelessness? Who decides who gets the condo and who gets the cardboard box?"

"The pain of being homeless—the endless waiting in welfare offices, the thoughtless dismissal, the terror of the streets, the endlessness of the long, dreary days, especially Sundays. The burdensome struggle to carry everything you own with you, the desperation of loneliness, the fear when the sun goes down, the biting cold of a careless February afternoon. The longing to have just five minutes alone with your kid for just one night, the distant memory of shared moments of joy and peace a long, long time ago. These are all real things that happen to real people."

"Justice is not three hots and a cot. Justice is having your own key."

"Homeless women are the survivors of a terrible war on the poor. We have accommodated ourselves to a world of alternatives instead of options. The only alternative to homelessness is a home, and the only alternative to hunger is food on your table."

"I can remember a Saturday night just before the Christmas holidays. An elderly woman on crutches watched me as I hung Christmas bulbs and holly around the dining room. She said—to no one in particular—'It was always Christmas for somebody else.' And I said to her, 'Not this year—this year we party!' And she smiled softly."

"Bigotry kills. It kills the spirit, the initiative, the ego, the mind, the body, and eventually the soul."

"We are accountable to and for each other. . . . We cannot hope to survive without contact with each other."

Other quotations from Kip Tiernan:
"Never forget that charity is scraps from the table and justice is a seat at the table. Charity is giving to others what belongs to you. Justice is giving to others what belongs to them."

"The rage I feel around homelessness and hunger and deprivation is barely containable. It is on the surface of my skin, my bones, and it lies coiled, ready to spring at a moment's notice. . . . Sometimes all you need is just plain stubborn hope."

"I sometimes wish everyone could experience the alienation and discrimination, the isolation of disapproval . . . so everyone could know how it feels to be unloved, unwanted, unnecessary."

"I have chosen the edge as my personal geography."

Source Notes

"Thank you. . . . when I was a child": "Kip Tiernan: A Legacy of Love," Rosie's Place, October 25, 2011, YouTube video, https://youtu.be/L4bDCDHbntQ.

All Kip Tiernan quotations in the text are from the Papers of Kip Tiernan 1994–2008, housed at the Schlesinger Library, Radcliffe Institute.